KU-414-101

THE FONDUE
COOKBOOK

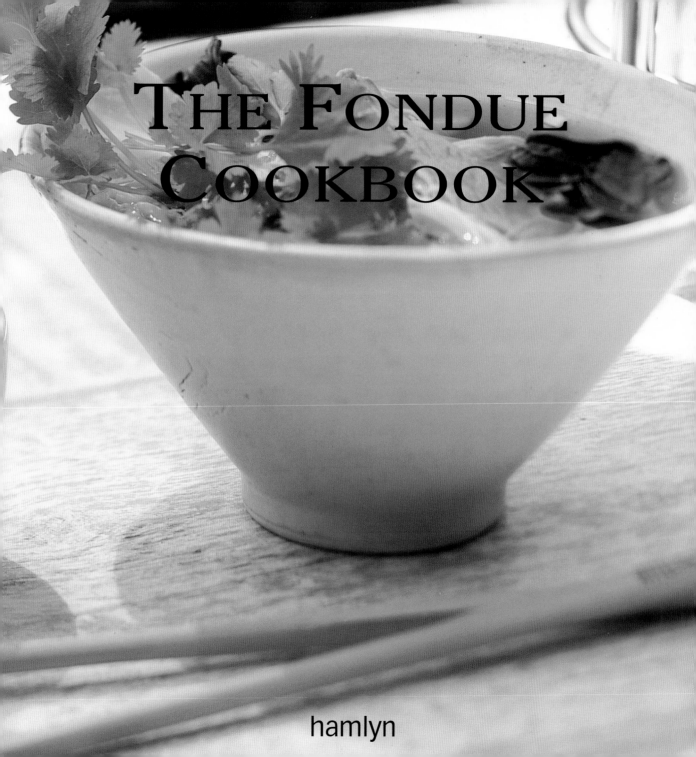

THE FONDUE
COOKBOOK

hamlyn

First published in 2001
by Hamlyn, a division of Octopus Publishing Group Limited
2–4 Heron Quays, London, E14 4JP

Copyright © 2001 Octopus Publishing Group Limited

All rights reserved. No part of this publication may be reproduced,
stored in a retrieval system or transmitted in any form
or by any means, electronic, mechanical, photocopying,
recording or otherwise, without the prior written permission of the publisher.

ISBN 0 600 60441 1

A CIP catalogue record for this book is available from the British Library

Printed and bound in China

Photographer: Sean Myers
Home Economist: Louise Pickford

NOTES

1 Eggs should be large unless otherwise stated. This book contains some dishes
made with raw or lightly cooked eggs. It is prudent for more vulnerable people,
such as pregnant and nursing mothers, invalids, the elderly, babies and young
children, to avoid uncooked or lightly cooked dishes made with eggs.

2 Both metric and imperial measures have been given in all recipes. Use one set
of measurements only and not a mix of both.

3 Cooking times are based on stove-top cooking and not the total tabletop
cooking unless otherwise stated.

4 This book contains dishes made with nuts and nut derivatives. It is advisable
for those with known allergic reactions to nuts and nut derivatives and those
who may be potentially vulnerable to these allergies, such as pregnant and nursing mothers, invalids, the elderly, babies and young children, to avoid dishes
made with nuts and nut oils. It is also prudent to check the labels of pre-
prepared ingredients for the possible inclusion of nut derivatives.

Contents

INTRODUCTION

When you think of informal and convivial ways to entertain guests, a fondue party immediately springs to mind. The word fondue comes from the French *fondre*, meaning 'to melt' or 'to blend', as originally this Swiss national dish was made with cheese melted in wine. Fondues have recently had a resurgence of interest, and it's easy to see why. A fondue is an easy dish to serve at a casual lunch or dinner party, where it can be used either as a main course or a dessert (or even both). Sauces and accompaniments can be as few or as many as you like. Since most of the preparation can be done in advance, you can have more time to spend with your guests. And because so many ingredients lend themselves to fondue-making, you can create a diverse range of dishes, both savoury and sweet.

History and Traditions

There are many stories about the origin of fondue, but the one told most often attributes its invention to isolated villagers living in Alpine regions who, during a long, harsh winter, subsisted on what they had to hand – cheese (that grew harder and harder), homemade bread (that became stale) and wine. They christened the dish *fondue au fromage*. The first fondues were made with Emmental and Gruyère cheese and were cooked in a heavy earthenware pan called a *caquelon*, which ensured that the cheese melted slowly and did not become lumpy or stringy. This creamy mixture was eaten with skewered pieces of French bread. Later, other dishes were derived from the traditional cheese fondue: these included *fondue bourguignonne* (from the French beef *bourguignonne* from Burgundy), a meat-based fondue that is cooked in stock or in hot oil, and dessert fondues, which are often but not exclusively made with chocolate and a liqueur.

The Chinese also have their own version of fondue. Introduced to the Far East by the Mongols in the fourteenth century, their fondue was originally made with mutton, *bourguignonne*-style, in a fondue pot over a special charcoal burner that is incorporated into it. Nowadays strips of meat (beef and pork), slices of chicken, pieces of fish and chicken stock are used.

There are a number of traditions associated with eating a fondue. The Swiss prefer to drink Kirsch or Chasselas, a dry white wine, with their cheese fondues, and share among all the guests the delicious cheese crust that is left in the pot. They then serve grilled sausages and crisp apples or pears for the next course. Another Swiss custom is the forfeit: if a woman drops a bread cube into the fondue, she has to kiss all the men; if a man drops the bread cube, he has to buy a bottle of wine for each guest. And if anyone drops a bread cube for a second time, he or she must host the next fondue party.

Equipment

There are different types of fondue pots, and it is important to use the correct one for your chosen dish. Alternatively, if you only want to buy a single pot, choose one that is made of stainless steel or copper with a removable porcelain insert. The fondue pot with the insert can be used for cheese or chocolate fondues; the fondue pot without the insert can be used for *fondue bourguignonne* and its variations.

Pots for cheese fondues

These are either made of glazed earthenware or ceramic-lined metal, metal (stainless steel or copper) with a porcelain insert, or cast iron. These pots are thick, heavy and shallow, and their slow transmission of heat helps prevent the cheese from burning.

Pots for meat, poultry, fish and vegetable fondues

These are usually made of stainless steel, copper or cast iron and are larger than cheese-fondue pots. The metal transmits heat quickly and helps keep the liquid, usually stock or oil, at a high temperature.

Pots for dessert fondues

These are made of stainless steel and copper and should have a porcelain insert.

Many fondue pots are sold as boxed sets, which include a stand, a burner, long two-pronged metal skewers (frequently with colour-coded handles so diners know which one is theirs) and sometimes a cork mat to go under the stand to protect the table. Depending upon the type of burner you have, you can use solid fuel in packets that are made to fit into the burner, or methylated spirit. Electric fondue pots are also available. Always follow the manufacturer's instructions for preparing and caring for your fondue pot so that it will last for many years.

Cheese fondues

Cheeses have varying fat and moisture levels, and therefore react differently to heat, so it is important to choose the correct type of cheese for making a fondue. Use a cheese or combination of cheeses that is good for melting, and yields a smooth and creamy consistency. The best cheeses are Emmental, Gruyère, Fontina, Pecorino, Provolone, Parmesan, Vacherin, Gouda, Edam and Cheddar. However, many other cheeses have been used successfully in fondue recipes, including mature Comté, Appenzell, Tilsit, Beaufort, Camembert, Pont l'Evêque and Livarot, to name a few. If you use a cheese with a low-fat content, you may need to add a knob of butter to the mixture to prevent the cheese from sticking to the pot. Always use a good-quality mature cheese: if the cheese is not aged or is poorly aged, it won't melt smoothly.

Heat is vital, too: if it is too intense, the cheese will become stringy and the fondue will be spoiled. The heat must also be carefully controlled; this is easily done by adjusting the heat control on the burner.

It is traditional to rub the inside of the fondue pot with a piece of cut garlic before adding the wine. This gives the fondue a subtle savoury flavour. As the cheese melts in the hot wine, add a little lemon juice; its acidity will help to melt the cheese completely. You can also add Kirsch, mixed with a little cornflour as a thickener. Stir the mixture with a wooden spoon, using a figure-of-eight motion, for a smooth blend. When the pot is set over the burner, adjust the heat so that the fondue bubbles gently. Never rush cheese fondues as slow cooking gives the best results.

If the fondue becomes too thick, add a little warmed wine; if it is too thin, add a little cornflour. If the fondue separates and becomes lumpy, place the pot on the hob over a moderate heat and whisk gently. Blend a little cornflour with a drop of wine and stir it into the fondue.

Dry white wine is nearly always used in cheese fondues, with Kirsch, beer and Champagne as tasty alternatives in some recipes.

French bread is the traditional dipper for cheese fondues. If the crust is kept on and the bread is one day old, spearing will be easier. Other breads to use include pitta, grissini, brown or rye bread cubes, or indeed any bread that would complement the dish. However it is not necessary to limit yourself to bread: many recipes call for prawns or salami or, for a lighter meal, raw vegetables. Sauces are unnecessary, but if you like you can accompany rich cheese fondues with a tossed green salad.

Kirsch and Chasselas are the drinks of choice for the Swiss (with tea as an alternative), but you do not have to follow their example. Among the best wines to accompany a cheese fondue are dry whites such as Chablis, Hock, Riesling or Alsatian Pinot Gris, or a Californian Chardonnay or a New World Sauvignon. For a wonderful variation, try the red Chinon.

Beer makes a good accompaniment to a beer-cheese fondue and, for a special occasion, Champagne for a Champagne-cheese fondue (see pages 33 and 32).

Meat, poultry, fish and vegetable fondues
Meat and chicken fondues
With meat and chicken fondues, it is best to heat the cooking liquid on the hob before bringing the pot to the table. For oil, the temperature needs to be 190°C (375°F), or when a bread cube browns in 30 seconds. Stock should be at boiling point.

The best cuts of meat result in a more tender, flavoursome and quickly cooked meat fondue. Fillet or sirloin steak is the basis for the traditional *bourguignonne*, but pork and lamb fillet make tasty alternatives. These meats can either be cut into bite-sized pieces or into slices (see the tip for slicing meat in Mongolian Lamb Hot Pot on page 42). If you like, you can marinate the meat first for extra flavour. You can also make a novel fondue with meatballs (see page 48).

Don't let meat or poultry fall to the bottom of the pot as it can stick. And don't overfill the pot – the oil may bubble up and overflow.

The tastiest and most tender poultry to use is skinned breast meat. The meat can either be sliced thinly into strips or slivers or cut into bite-sized pieces.

The liquid for meat and chicken fondues is usually chicken stock but, depending on the dish, consommé and even coconut milk (for a Thai fondue) can be used.

Meat fondues especially, but also poultry ones, can be enlivened with sauces, relishes, chutneys, mayonnaises, mustards and ketchups. The recipes in this book suggest a selection of accompaniments, but again you can prepare many others that will make good partners for your chosen ingredients. Chinese fondues can be made into a real feast with the addition of rice or noodles, and even spring rolls (see page 46).

For a flavoursome meat-based fondue such as Fondue Bourguignonne (see page 50), offer a full-bodied red wine such as Californian or Coonawarra Cabernet, or a Burgundy or Bordeaux. White or red wines both go well with poultry. The more basic dishes can have a French *vin de pays*, going up the scale to an oaked Chardonnay, and on to reds like Bergerac.

Fish fondues

Firm fish and shellfish are best for fish fondues, although flaked fish such as crab will add a delicate touch to the dish. Flat fish need to be boned and the skin removed before being cut into bite-sized pieces. Prawns should be peeled, mussels shelled and squid cleaned and cut into pieces. Dry white wine is especially good for fish fondues; a dash of brandy adds another level of flavour. Oil is used for deep-frying.

Fish fondues are often lighter, with the shellfish such as prawns and mussels used as a dipper. French bread and pitta breads are other alternatives, as are puff pastry crescents and cheese straws. Tartare sauce and a salad would complete the meal.

As an accompaniment, shellfish fondues will benefit from wines that are crisp, dry and white, such as a Muscadet sur lie, Chablis, New World Sauvignon Blanc, or an unoaked or lightly oaked Chardonnay.

Vegetable fondues

Almost any vegetable can be used for a fondue, but it is best to choose those that can be eaten in one or two bites. If baby vegetables are not available, use whole vegetables (button mushrooms, shallots, mangetouts, radishes) or cut the vegetables into strips or sticks (carrots, celery), slices (courgettes), pieces (asparagus tips or spears) and florets (broccoli, cauliflower).

Vegetables can make up the fondue itself or be used as dippers. Or you can follow serving suggestions for a cheese fondue, such as salami or corn chips. For a treat, try the sauce that accompanies Tempura (see page 30).

White wine is perfect to accompany vegetable fondues. Try one that is crisp, dry, and aromatic such as an Australian Riesling or a Vouvray.

Dessert fondues

When preparing a chocolate-based fondue, always follow the recipe directions. It may be necessary to put water into the pot before it is placed on the burner, thereby creating a water bath (*bain-marie*) that will keep the chocolate from burning. Dessert fondues can be cooked with liqueurs, fruit juices and cream.

Although chocolate and orange are a classic combination, almost any fruit can be used in these fondues. Chunks of banana, pineapple, peach, nectarine and plum, and whole raspberries, strawberries and cherries are all delicious. These fondues can also be served with langues de chat biscuits, macaroons, sweet biscuits, sponge fingers and marshmallows.

Dessert wines and liqueurs are preferable with these fondues. If one of them is used in the fondue itself, you can serve it, on the rocks for example, with the dish.

Party planning

Fondue parties work best if there are no more than six people at the table as a fondue pot only holds a certain amount of food. However, for a fondue buffet, you can borrow a second pot and make two different fondues, one meat and one vegetable, for example. Warn guests that food from the pot is very hot, and that they should not eat it immediately from the skewers or they will burn their tongues.

For advance preparation, cut the bread into chunks and serve in baskets, set out the dipping sauces in separate bowls. For a Chinese fondue, you'll need soup bowls and spoons to drink the stock, and perhaps chopsticks. For dessert fondues with fruit, prepare all the fruit just before the party begins, squeeze over some lemon juice to prevent the fruit from turning brown, and heap into serving bowls. Serve with bamboo skewers.

TRADITIONAL CHEESE FONDUE (NEUCHÂTEL FONDUE)

I garlic clove, halved
150 ml (¼ pint) dry white wine
I teaspoon lemon juice
300 g (10 oz) Emmental cheese, grated
300 g (10 oz) Gruyère cheese, grated
I tablespoon cornflour
3 tablespoons Kirsch
pinch of white pepper
pinch of ground nutmeg
pinch of paprika
cubes of French bread, to serve

1 Rub the inside of a fondue pot with the cut garlic, then discard the garlic. Pour the wine into the pan with the lemon juice and heat gently. Gradually add the Emmental and Gruyère, stirring in a figure-of-eight motion, until all the cheese is combined.
2 Blend the cornflour with the Kirsch and add to the fondue when the mixture begins to bubble. Continue to cook gently for a further 2–3 minutes, then season according to taste with the pepper, nutmeg and paprika.
3 Transfer the fondue pot to the table and keep warm over a burner. Serve with cubes of French bread to dip into the fondue.

Serves 4
Preparation time: 10 minutes
Cooking time: 15–20 minutes

GORGONZOLA AND GRUYÈRE FONDUE

250 g (8 oz) Gorgonzola or other blue
cheese, grated or crumbled
250 g (8 oz) Gruyère cheese, grated
20 g (¼ oz) plain flour
250 ml (8 fl oz) dry white wine
I garlic clove, crushed
75 ml (2½ fl oz) Kirsch
pinch of nutmeg
pepper

To serve:
cubes of toasted bread
celery stalks, trimmed
carrot sticks
chicory leaves

1 Mix the Gorgonzola and Gruyère cheeses with the flour. Heat the wine and garlic in a fondue pot on the hob.

2 Add the cheese mixture gradually to the pan, stirring constantly and allowing each addition to melt before adding more. When you have added all the cheese and the mixture is smooth, stir in the Kirsch and nutmeg and season to taste with pepper.

3 Transfer the fondue pot to the table and keep it warm over a burner. Serve with cubes of toasted bread, celery stalks, carrot sticks and chicory leaves to dip into the fondue.

Serves 4
Preparation time: 15 minutes
Cooking time: 15–20 minutes

THREE CHEESE FONDUE

1 garlic clove, halved
50 g (2 oz) butter
1–2 celery sticks, finely chopped
300 ml (½ pint) dry white wine
375 g (12 oz) Emmental cheese, grated
375 g (12 oz) Gruyère cheese, grated
50 g (2 oz) Parmesan cheese, grated
pinch of dry mustard
pinch of nutmeg
pinch of cayenne pepper
1 tablespoon cornflour
2 tablespoons brandy

To serve:
large cooked peeled prawns
cubes of French bread

1 Rub the inside of a fondue pot with the cut clove of garlic, then discard the garlic. Add the butter and allow to melt. Add the celery and fry for 5–10 minutes. Stir in the wine and heat gently.
2 Gradually add the three grated cheeses, stirring until melted. Season with the mustard, nutmeg and cayenne pepper. Blend the cornflour with the brandy and stir into the fondue. Bring to the boil and cook for 10 minutes, stirring all the time.
3 Transfer the fondue pot to the table and keep warm over a burner. Serve with large prawns and cubes of French bread to dip into the fondue.

Serves 4
Preparation time: 10–15 minutes
Cooking time: 30 minutes

DUTCH FONDUE

Many years ago, the farmers' wives in Holland used cheeses which were not perfect in shape for making fondue. Dutch gin was the preferred flavouring, but in this recipe Kirsch, whisky, brandy or sherry could be used instead.

½ garlic clove
150 ml (¼ pint) dry white wine
1 teaspoon lemon juice
425 g (14 oz) Gouda or Edam cheese, grated
1 tablespoon cornflour
1½ tablespoons Dutch gin
pinch of nutmeg
pepper

To serve:
cubes of French bread
green salad (optional)

1 Rub the inside of a fondue pot with the cut garlic clove, then discard the garlic. Pour in the wine and lemon juice and heat slowly until the wine is nearly boiling. Add the grated cheese a little at a time, stirring continuously with a fork, until all the cheese has melted.

2 Blend the cornflour smoothly with the gin and, when the cheese mixture boils, stir in the blended cornflour. Add a pinch of pepper and a pinch of nutmeg.

3 Transfer the fondue pot to the table and keep warm over a burner. Serve with cubes of French bread for dipping, and accompany with a tossed green salad, if liked.

Serves 4
Preparation time: 10 minutes
Cooking time: 20 minutes

ITALIAN FONDUE

An Italian cheese such as Pecorino or Provolone should be used in this fondue. Pecorino cheeses are made from ewes' milk while Provolone comes in a variety of shapes and has a strong flavour. If neither is available, use Parmesan.

1 garlic clove, halved
300 ml (½ pint) dry white wine
1 teaspoon lemon juice
500 g (1 lb) Pecorino, Provolone or Parmesan cheese, grated
2 tablespoons cornflour
4 tablespoons Kirsch or dry sherry
cubes of Italian or French bread, to serve

1 Rub the inside of a fondue pot with the cut clove of garlic, then discard the garlic. Add the wine and lemon juice and warm over a low heat.

2 Add the cheese gradually and stir until it has melted, keeping the heat low. Mix the cornflour thoroughly with the Kirsch, add to the cheese mixture and stir until the fondue bubbles and is thick and creamy.

3 Transfer the fondue pot to the table and keep warm over a burner. Serve with cubes of Italian or French bread to dip into the fondue.

Serves 4–5
Preparation time: 10 minutes
Cooking time: 20 minutes

FRESH HERB FONDUE

1 garlic clove, halved
150 ml (¼ pint) dry white wine
500 g (1 lb) Gruyère cheese, grated
1 tablespoon cornflour
1 tablespoon chopped parsley
1 tablespoon chopped chives
1 tablespoon chopped oregano
salt and pepper

To serve:
cubes of French bread
chunks of salami

1 Rub the inside of a fondue pot with the cut garlic clove, then discard the garlic. Pour in the wine and heat gently, then add the cheese and stir continuously until melted. Blend the cornflour with a little water and add to the fondue with the herbs and salt and pepper to taste. Heat until thickened, stirring well.
2 Transfer the fondue pot to the table and keep warm over a burner. Serve with French bread and chunks of salami to dip into the fondue.

Serves 4
Preparation time: 10 minutes
Cooking time: 15 minutes

GENEVA FONDUE

This rich, thin fondue is generally eaten with noodles. Cook them and keep them hot while making the fondue.

8 egg yolks
250 g (8 oz) Gruyère cheese, grated
a little grated nutmeg
125 g (4 oz) butter
150 ml (¼ pint) double cream
salt and pepper
noodles, to serve

1 Beat the egg yolks and put them into the fondue pot with the cheese, nutmeg and salt and pepper to taste.

2 When the cheese has melted, add the butter a little at a time and stir continuously over a gentle heat.

3 When the mixture thickens, add the cream. Stir for a few minutes longer then pour over the noodles.

Serves 3–4
Preparation time: 10 minutes
Cooking time: 20 minutes

BERNESE FONDUE

This fondue contains a mixture of cheeses including Sbrinz, probably the oldest Swiss hard cheese, from the south Central Alps region. If you cannot find it use Parmesan instead.

1 garlic clove, halved
50 g (2 oz) butter
2–3 shallots
50 g (2 oz) button mushrooms
½ bottle dry white wine
375 g (12 oz) grated Emmental cheese
375 g (12 oz) grated Gruyère cheese
50 g (2 oz) grated Sbrinz or Parmesan cheese
¼ teaspoon mustard powder
¼ teaspoon paprika
¼ teaspoon grated nutmeg
1 tablespoon cornflour
2 tablespoons dry sherry
salt and pepper
cubes of French bread, to serve

1 Rub the cut clove of garlic round the inside of the fondue pot, then discard the garlic. Add the butter and when it has melted add the shallots and mushrooms and cook for 5–10 minutes.

2 Stir in the white wine and when it is hot but not boiling add the three cheeses and stir continuously until melted. Add the mustard, paprika and nutmeg and season with salt and pepper.

3 Blend the cornflour smoothly with the sherry and add to the fondue. Stir until almost boiling, then simmer for about 15 minutes stirring constantly with a figure-of-eight motion.

4 Transfer the fondue pot to the table and keep warm over a burner. Serve with cubes of French bread to dip into the fondue.

Serves 4–5
Preparation time: 10 minutes
Cooking time: 35–40 minutes

AVOCADO FONDUE

25 g (1 oz) butter
1 onion, finely chopped
4 tablespoons plain flour
250 ml (8 fl oz) milk
4 tablespoons lemon juice
1 avocado, mashed or liquidized (skin and stone removed)
50 g (2 oz) Emmental or Gruyère cheese, grated
150 ml (¼ pint) single cream
few drops of Tabasco sauce
salt and pepper

To serve:
cherry or vine tomatoes
cubes of French bread
large cooked peeled prawns

1 Melt the butter in a fondue pot, add the onion and fry until softened. Stir in the flour and cook for 2 minutes. Remove the pan from the heat and add the milk, lemon juice and avocado and season with salt and pepper.

2 Cook gently for 5 minutes, stirring all the time and taking care not to let the mixture boil. Add the cheese and stir until melted. Stir in the cream and Tabasco sauce.

3 Transfer the fondue pot to the table and keep warm over a burner. Serve immediately with the tomatoes with the stems attached for dipping, cubes of French bread and large prawns to dip into the fondue.

Serves 4
Preparation time: 10 minutes
Cooking time: 20–25 minutes

ONION AND CARAWAY FONDUE

If you find the flavour of caraway seeds too strong, try using fennel seeds or lightly toasted sesame seeds instead.

50 g (2 oz) butter
250 g (8 oz) onions, chopped
2 teaspoons caraway seeds
300 ml (½ pint) dry white wine
375 g (12 oz) Gruyère cheese, grated
375 g (12 oz) Emmental cheese, grated
1 teaspoon wholegrain mustard
pinch of grated nutmeg
1 tablespoon cornflour
2 tablespoons dry vermouth
cubes of French bread, to serve

1 Melt the butter in a fondue pot and fry the onion and caraway seeds for 5–10 minutes, until soft but not browned.

2 Pour in the wine and heat gently. Gradually add the Gruyère and Emmental cheeses, stirring continuously until melted. Stir in the mustard and nutmeg.

3 Blend the cornflour with the vermouth and stir into the fondue. Cook over a low heat until thickened, stirring continuously.

4 Transfer the fondue pot to the table and keep warm over a burner. Serve with cubes of bread to dip into the fondue.

Serves 4–6
Preparation time: 15–20 minutes
Cooking time: 25–30 minutes

SPRING VEGETABLE FONDUE

16 button mushrooms
16 cauliflower florets
16 broccoli florets
16 carrot sticks
16 tiny parboiled potatoes
16 courgette slices
vegetable oil, for deep-frying

Batter:
125 g (4 oz) plain flour, sifted
½ teaspoon salt
1 tablespoon corn oil
150 ml (¼ pint) water
2 egg whites

To serve:
Tomato Relish (see below) or a selection
of dipping sauces (see page 50)

1 Cut the vegetables into small pieces, so that they will cook quickly. Wash and pat dry with kitchen paper, to remove any excess moisture.
2 To prepare the batter, mix the flour and salt in a bowl and gradually add the oil and water, beating until smooth. Whisk the egg whites until they form stiff peaks and carefully fold them into the batter, just before it is required.
3 Half-fill a fondue pot with oil and heat on a hob to 180°C (350°F), or until a cube of bread browns in 40 seconds.
4 Transfer the fondue pot to the table and keep warm over a burner. To eat, spear pieces of vegetable on to long fondue forks and dip into the batter, coating completely. Cook in the oil until the batter is crisp and golden brown. Serve with Tomato Relish or another sauce. A mixed salad and French bread also go well.

Serves 4
Preparation time: about 30 minutes
Cooking time: 5–10 minutes

TOMATO RELISH

6 ripe tomatoes, skinned and chopped
6 red peppers, cored, deseeded and finely chopped
3 onions, finely chopped
2 red chillies, deseeded and finely chopped
450 ml (¾ pint) red wine vinegar
175 g (6 oz) soft light brown sugar
4 tablespoons mustard seeds
2 tablespoons celery seeds
1 tablespoon paprika
2 teaspoons salt
2 teaspoons pepper

1 Place all the ingredients in a large saucepan and bring slowly to the boil. Simmer, uncovered, for about 30 minutes until most of the liquid has evaporated and the relish has a thick, pulpy consistency. Stir frequently as the relish thickens.
2 Pour into clean, sterilized jars. (To sterilize the jars, put the clean jars, open end up, on a baking sheet and place in a preheated cool oven, 140°C (275°F), Gas Mark 1, for about 10 minutes until hot.) When the relish has cooled, seal with vinegar-proof covers.

Makes about 1.5 kg (3 lb)
Preparation time: 20 minutes
Cooking time: about 35 minutes

BAGNA CAUDA WITH SUMMER VEGETABLES

This is a classic warm oil, butter and anchovy dip found all over Italy and is the perfect accompaniment to your favourite sweet fragrant summer vegetables.

25 g (1 oz) unsalted butter
2 garlic cloves, crushed
50 g (2 oz) can anchovies in oil, drained and roughly chopped
125 ml (4 fl oz) olive oil
500 g (1 lb) prepared vegetable crudités (such as baby carrots, radishes, French beans, celery sticks)
French bread, to serve (optional)

1 Put the butter and garlic into a small saucepan and heat gently until the butter has melted. Simmer gently for 2 minutes but do not allow the butter or garlic to burn.
2 Stir in the anchovies and then gradually whisk in the oil. Continue to heat gently for 10 minutes, stirring from time to time. Pour into a heatproof bowl and serve at once with a selection of vegetable crudités and some crusty French bread, if wished.

Serves 4–6
Preparation time: 10 minutes, plus preparing vegetables
Cooking time: about 20 minutes

ASPARAGUS AND BLUE CHEESE FONDUE

8–10 asparagus spears
250 g (8 oz) blue cheese, crumbled
1 tablespoon plain flour
150 ml (¼ pint) dry white wine
150 ml (¼ pint) single cream
pepper

To serve:
cubes of ham
cubes of French bread
slices of salami

1 Trim any woody bases from the asparagus and peel them if necessary. Cook in lightly salted boiling water for 10–15 minutes until tender. Drain the asparagus and chop the spears into 1 cm (½ inch) pieces.

2 Mix together the cheese and flour. Heat the wine in a fondue pot until almost boiling. Add the cheese and flour mixture and stir constantly until thickened. Stir in the cream and season with pepper, then add the asparagus and heat gently for 3–4 minutes.

3 Transfer the fondue pot to the table and keep warm over a burner. Serve the fondue with cubes of ham, French bread and slices of salami for dipping.

Serves 4
Preparation time: 10 minutes
Cooking time: 30–35 minutes

BLUE CHEESE AND CHIVE FONDUE

1 garlic clove, halved
1 tablespoon cornflour
150 ml (¼ pint) white wine
250 g (8 oz) Stilton or Danish blue cheese,
crumbled
300 ml (½ pint) soured cream
1 tablespoon chopped parsley
2 tablespoons chopped chives
salt and pepper

To serve:
250 g (8 oz) baby new potatoes, boiled
125 g (4 oz) broccoli florets
125 g (4 oz) cauliflower florets

1 Rub the inside of a fondue pot with the cut garlic clove, then discard the garlic. Blend the cornflour with a little of the wine, add the remaining wine to the fondue pot, and bring to the boil. Add the cornflour mixture and cook, stirring constantly, until thickened.

2 Add the cheese and stir until melted, then add the soured cream, parsley and chives and season to taste with salt and pepper.

3 Transfer the fondue pot to the table and keep warm over a burner. Serve with new potatoes and broccoli and cauliflower florets to dip into the fondue.

Serves 4–6
Preparation time: 10–15 minutes
Cooking time: 20 minutes

TEMPURA

sunflower oil, for deep-frying
8 button mushrooms
I red pepper, cored, deseeded and sliced
lengthways into strips
4 courgettes, sliced into rounds

Batter:
150 g (5 oz) plain flour
2 tablespoons arrowroot or cornflour
pinch of salt
300 ml (½ pint) iced water

Dipping sauce:
4 tablespoons soy sauce
4 tablespoons dry sherry
I tablespoon finely chopped fresh root
ginger
pinch of mustard powder
½ teaspoon caster sugar

1 First make the batter. Sift the flour and arrowroot or cornflour into a bowl with the salt. Add the water a little at a time, whisking constantly. Cover and place in the refrigerator to chill for 30 minutes.

2 Meanwhile, whisk the dipping sauce ingredients in a bowl. Pour enough oil into a fondue pot for deep-frying and heat to 190°C (375°F) or until a cube of bread browns in 30 seconds.

3 Using a slotted spoon, dip a few pieces of each vegetable into the batter, then lift them out, making sure there is plenty of batter around them.

4 Transfer the fondue pot to the table and keep the oil hot over a burner. Lower the vegetables gently into the hot oil and deep-fry for 2–3 minutes until crisp. Lift out with a slotted spoon, drain on kitchen paper and keep hot while deep-frying the remainder.

5 Whisk the dipping sauce again, then divide it equally between 4 individual dipping bowls. Serve the tempura at once, with the bowls of dipping sauce on the side.

Serves 4
Preparation time: 10 minutes, plus chilling
Cooking time: 2–3 minutes for each batch

CHAMPAGNE FONDUE

65 g (2½ oz) mushroom caps
500 ml (17 fl oz) Champagne
500 g (1 lb) Gruyère cheese, grated
3 tablespoons plain flour
2 egg yolks
1 tablespoon cream
salt and pepper

To serve:
cubes of ham
cubes of French bread
cubes of cucumber

1 To prepare the mushrooms, cook them for 5 minutes in enough boiling water to cover. Drain, reserving 50 ml (2 fl oz) of the cooking liquid, then slice the mushrooms thinly.

2 Heat the Champagne slowly in a fondue pot on the hob. Stir in the cheese and flour and cook, stirring, until melted and smooth.

3 Combine the egg yolks, cream, the reserved cooking liquid and the mushrooms and stir into the fondue. Do not allow to boil. Season with salt and pepper to taste.

4 Transfer the fondue pot to the table and keep hot over a burner. Serve with cubes of ham, French bread and cucumber to dip into the fondue.

Serves 4
Preparation time: 20 minutes
Cooking time: 25 minutes

BEER AND ONION FONDUE

40 g (1½ oz) butter
1 onion, finely chopped
250 ml (8 fl oz) beer
250 g (8 oz) Cheddar cheese, grated
1 garlic clove, crushed
3 tablespoons cornflour
½ teaspoon mustard powder
pepper

To serve:
cubes of French bread
pickled onions

1 Heat ½ oz of the butter in a frying pan. Add the onion and fry gently until softened but not browned.
2 Put the beer, cheese, garlic and onion into a fondue pot. Cook gently, stirring, over a low heat on the hob until the cheese has melted. Stir in the remaining butter.
3 Blend the cornflour and mustard with a little water and add to the fondue pot. Continue cooking until the fondue has thickened, stirring constantly. Season with pepper to taste.
4 Transfer the fondue pot to the table and keep hot over a burner. Serve with cubes of French bread and pickled onions to dip into the fondue.

Serves 2
Preparation time: 10 minutes
Cooking time: 20 minutes

CHILI CON QUESO

25 g (1 oz) butter
50 g (2 oz) onions, chopped
1–2 garlic cloves, crushed
2–4 green or red chillies, deseeded and chopped
3–4 tablespoons chopped and deseeded jalapeño peppers
250 g (8 oz) tomatoes, peeled, deseeded and chopped
75 g (3 oz) cream cheese, cubed
250 g (8 oz) Cheddar cheese, grated
milk or single cream (optional)
salt
corn chips, to serve

1 Melt the butter in a fondue pot. Add the onions and garlic and cook gently, stirring occasionally, until softened. Add the chillies, jalapeños and tomatoes and cook, stirring, until the excess liquid has evaporated.

2 Add both cheeses and cook very gently, stirring, until the cheeses have melted. Do not let the mixture get too hot. Add salt to taste.

3 Transfer the fondue pot to the table and keep warm over a burner. Serve with corn chips for dipping. If the fondue becomes too thick, stir in a little milk or cream.

Serves 6–8
Preparation time: 10–15 minutes
Cooking time: about 30 minutes

SMOKED HADDOCK FONDUE

750 g (1½ lb) smoked haddock fillet
1 small onion, chopped
1 carrot, sliced
1 bouquet garni
5 peppercorns
small handful of parsley, chopped
300 ml (½ pint) dry white wine
salt and pepper

To serve:
tartare sauce
pitta bread
green salad

1 Skin the haddock. Cut it into bite-sized chunks and set aside. Place the fish trimmings in a saucepan with the onion, carrot, bouquet garni, peppercorns and parsley. Cover with cold water and bring to the boil, then simmer for 30 minutes. Strain the cooking liquid into a jug, season with salt and pepper and pour in the wine.

2 Pour the mixture into a fondue pot and bring to the boil. Transfer the fondue pot to the table and keep hot over a burner.

3 To eat, spear a chunk of haddock on to a fondue fork and dip into the boiling stock until cooked. Serve with tartare sauce, pitta bread and a green salad.

Serves 4
Preparation time: 15 minutes
Cooking time: 35 minutes

PRAWN AND CHEESE FONDUE

1 garlic clove, halved
25 g (1 oz) butter
2 shallots, chopped
65 g (2½ oz) mushrooms, finely chopped
150 ml (¼ pint) dry white wine
175 g (6 oz) Gruyère cheese, grated
175 g (6 oz) Cheddar cheese, grated
3 teaspoons cornflour
2 tablespoons brandy
125 g (4 oz) cooked peeled prawns
50 ml (2 fl oz) single cream
salt and pepper

To serve:
cubes of toasted French bread
celery stalks, trimmed
red pepper strips

1 Rub the inside of a fondue pot with the cut clove of garlic, then discard the garlic. Melt the butter in the pot on the hob, add the shallots and fry until soft. Add the mushrooms and fry for 2 minutes. Pour in the wine and heat gently until nearly boiling. Gradually add the Gruyère and Cheddar cheeses and stir constantly until they have melted.

2 Blend the cornflour with the brandy and add to the pan, then stir until thickened. Add the prawns and cream and season with salt and pepper. Reduce the heat and cook for 3–4 minutes until the prawns have heated through.

3 Transfer the fondue pot to the table and keep warm over a burner. Serve with cubes of toasted bread, celery stalks and strips of red pepper to dip into the fondue.

Serves 4
Preparation time: 10–15 minutes
Cooking time: 30–40 minutes

SEAFOOD AND WHITE WINE FONDUE

Use a wide fondue pot for this dish, similar to one used for making a cheese fondue.

375 g (12 oz) white fish fillet
125 g (4 oz) self-raising flour
generous pinch of salt
I egg
150 ml (¼ pint) water
oil, for deep-frying

Fondue:
65 g (2½ oz) butter
65 g (2½ oz) plain flour
300 ml (½ pint) fish stock
450 ml (¾ pint) dry white wine
150 ml (¼ pint) double cream
3 egg yolks
salt and pepper

To serve:
175 g (6 oz) large cooked peeled prawns
hot French bread

I Cut the fish fillet into 2 cm (¾ inch) cubes.

2 Sift the self-raising flour and salt into a bowl. Add the egg and a little of the water and beat until smooth. Beat in the remaining water until well combined.

3 Dip each piece of fish into the batter to give an even coating. Fill a deep pan one-third full with oil and heat to 190°C (375°F), or until a cube of bread browns in 30 seconds. Lower the fish into the hot oil and fry for about 3 minutes until crisp and golden. Drain on kitchen paper. (The crispy fish pieces can be prepared up to an hour in advance and then crisped up in a moderately hot oven.)

4 To make the fondue, melt the butter in a fondue pot and stir in the flour. Cook for 1 minute, stirring. Gradually stir in the fish stock and wine, whisking until the sauce is smooth. Add salt and pepper to taste.

5 Pour the wine sauce into a fondue pot, then transfer the pot to the table and keep warm over a burner.

6 Beat the cream with the egg yolks and stir into the hot wine sauce. Take care that the fondue does not boil at this stage.

7 Divide the crispy fish pieces and prawns between 4 individual plates. Thread on to bamboo skewers or fondue forks and dip into the fondue. Accompany with chunks of hot French bread.

Serves 4
Preparation time: 25 minutes
Cooking time: 25 minutes

SMOKED MUSSEL FONDUE

I garlic clove, halved
150 ml (5 fl oz) dry white wine
500 g (1 lb) Emmental cheese, grated
1 tablespoon cornflour
1 tablespoon chopped parsley
1 tablespoon dry sherry
125 g (4 oz) can smoked mussels
salt and pepper
cubes of French bread, to serve

1 Rub the inside of a fondue pot with the cut garlic clove, then discard the garlic. Pour the wine into the fondue pot and heat gently on the hob.

2 Gradually add the cheese and cornflour, stirring continuously until all the cheese has melted. Stir in the parsley, sherry and mussels. Season with salt and pepper and heat until thickened.

3 Transfer the fondue pot to the table and keep warm over a burner. Serve with cubes of French bread to dip into the fondue.

Serves 4
Preparation time: 10 minutes
Cooking time: 20 minutes

CRAB FONDUE

1 garlic clove, halved
300 ml (½ pint) dry white wine
300 g (10 oz) mild Cheddar cheese, grated
1 tablespoon plain flour
175 g (6 oz) white crab meat, flaked
salt and pepper
puff pastry crescents or cheese straws,
to serve

1 Rub the inside of a fondue pot with the garlic clove, then discard the garlic.

2 Pour the white wine into the fondue pot. Heat on the hob until the wine just reaches boiling point.

3 Mix the grated cheese with the flour and add to the hot wine, whisking or stirring until smooth. Season with salt and pepper to taste and stir in the crab meat.

4 Transfer the fondue pot to the table and keep warm over a burner. Serve with crescents of puff pastry or cheese straws to dip into the fondue.

Serves 2–3
Preparation time: 10 minutes
Cooking time: 20 minutes

MONGOLIAN LAMB HOT POT

1 kg (2 lb) piece frozen lamb fillet
50 g (2 oz) transparent noodles
1 large Chinese cabbage, separated
into leaves
500 g (1 lb) spinach
2 cakes bean curd, thinly sliced
3 x 425 g (14 oz) cans consommé

Dipping sauces:
6 spring onions, finely chopped
2 tablespoons shredded root ginger
6 tablespoons sesame seed paste (tahini)
3 tablespoons sesame seed oil
6 tablespoons soy sauce
4 tablespoons chilli sauce
4 tablespoons chopped coriander leaves
(optional)

1 Allow the lamb to defrost slightly but, while it is still partially frozen, cut it into paper-thin slices, arrange them on a serving dish and leave to thaw completely.

2 Soak the noodles in hot water for 10 minutes then drain thoroughly.

3 Place the cabbage leaves and spinach in a serving dish. Arrange the bean curd and noodles on another dish.

4 To make the dipping sauces, combine the spring onions and ginger in a small bowl. Mix the sesame seed paste and oil in another bowl. Pour the soy sauce and chilli sauce into individual sauce bowls. If liked, serve some chopped coriander in another small bowl.

5 Heat the consommé in a saucepan on the hob until boiling. Pour it into a fondue pot (or a Chinese Fondue or Shabu, as shown). Transfer to the table and keep warm over a burner.

6 To serve, each diner first mixes his own sauce in a small dish. Using chopsticks, fondue forks or long skewers, each person dips a slice of meat into the hot consommé to cook, then dips it into his prepared sauce to eat.

7 When all the meat has been eaten, the vegetables, bean curd and noodles are added to the pot and cooked for about 5–10 minutes, and then the soup is ready to serve.

Serves 4–6
Preparation time: 35 minutes
Cooking time: 10–15 minutes

CHINESE FONDUE

1 litre (1¾ pints) chicken stock
1 onion, thinly sliced
1 large carrot, sliced
1 celery stick, chopped
4 large mushrooms, sliced
3 slices fresh root ginger

To dip:
175 g (6 oz) tiny button mushrooms
1 Chinese cabbage, shredded
½ small cauliflower, divided into tiny florets
125 g (4 oz) mangetouts or a handful of small spinach leaves
125 g (4 oz) cooked peeled prawns
175 g (6 oz) boneless, skinless chicken, cut into thin strips
175 g (6 oz) calves' liver, cut into thin strips
175 g (6 oz) beef fillet, cut into thin strips
175 g (6 oz) pork fillet, cut into thin strips

To serve:
accompanying sauces (see right)
boiled rice or noodles

1 Put the stock into a saucepan with the onion, carrot, celery, sliced mushrooms and ginger. Simmer gently for 10 minutes.

2 Arrange the prepared mushrooms, cabbage, cauliflower, mangetout, prawns, chicken, liver, beef and pork on a platter.

3 Transfer the stock to a Chinese Fondue (Shabu) or a fondue pot and keep warm over a burner.

4 To serve, provide each person with several little bowls of sauces for dipping and a bowl of hot boiled rice or noodles.

Sauces for Chinese Fondue

Soy and garlic sauce:
Put 150 ml (¼ pint) soy sauce into a pan with 3 finely chopped garlic cloves and simmer for 1–2 minutes. Serve warm or cold.

Plum sauce:
Mix 6 tablespoons plum jam with 2 tablespoons vinegar and 2 tablespoons chopped mango chutney. Serve cold. (If the jam is too chunky, push it through a sieve). Alternatively, you can buy plum sauce from Chinese food shops and some supermarkets.

Spring onion sauce:
Mix 6 tablespoons olive oil with 3 finely chopped spring onions, 1 crushed garlic clove, 1 tablespoon sesame seeds and salt and pepper to taste.

Lime and pepper sauce:
Mix the juice of 2 limes with 1 finely chopped red pepper, 1 finely chopped small onion, 3 tablespoons olive oil and salt and pepper to taste.

Serves 4–6
Preparation time: 40 minutes
Cooking time: 10–15 minutes

PORK SATAY FONDUE

750 g (1½ lb) lean pork fillet
vegetable oil, for deep-frying
Satay Sauce (see below), to serve

Marinade:
300 ml (½ pint) coconut milk
2 slices fresh root ginger
1 teaspoon ground coriander
1 teaspoon turmeric
1 teaspoon dark soft brown sugar
salt and pepper

1 Cut the meat into bite-sized pieces. Mix together all the marinade ingredients and marinate the meat overnight. Drain and dry on kitchen paper.
2 Half-fill a fondue pot with oil and heat gently on the hob to 190°C (375°F), or until a cube of bread browns in 30 seconds. Transfer the fondue pot to the table and keep warm over a burner.
3 Give each person a portion of the meat. They spear the meat on to a fondue fork and place it in the hot oil until it is cooked. Serve with the sauce, for dipping.

Serves 4
Preparation time: 20 minutes, plus marinating
Cooking time: 5 minutes

SATAY SAUCE

2 onions
2 tablespoons oil
75 g (3 oz) roasted peanuts
½ teaspoon chilli powder
150 ml (¼ pint) warm water
15 g (½ oz) soft brown sugar
1–2 tablespoons soy sauce
2 tablespoons lemon juice
salt

1 Slice one of the onions and fry it in the oil. Roughly chop the second onion and put it in a food processor or blender with the peanuts and chilli powder and blend until it forms a paste.
2 Add this paste to the fried onion and cook for a few minutes. Gradually stir in the water and sugar and cook for 2 minutes. Season to taste with soy sauce, lemon juice and salt, and heat through gently.

Serves 4
Preparation time: 10 minutes
Cooking time: about 12 minutes

MINIATURE SPRING ROLLS

125 g (4 oz) plain flour
about 40 g (1½ oz) cornflour
½ teaspoon salt
I egg
200 ml (7 fl oz) water
I egg white, lightly beaten, for brushing
oil, for deep-frying
salt and pepper
spring onion and red pepper curls, to
garnish (optional)

Filling:
175 g (6 oz) cooked chicken, minced
I tablespoon soy sauce
4 Chinese cabbage leaves, finely shredded
3 spring onions, finely chopped
4 canned water chestnuts, finely chopped
salt and pepper

Sweet and sour sauce:
4 tablespoons red wine vinegar
4 tablespoons brown sugar
300 ml (½ pint) chicken stock
I tablespoon tomato purée
2 teaspoons soy sauce
2 tablespoons cornflour
3 tablespoons cold water

I Sift the flour, cornflour and salt into a bowl. Make a well in the centre. Add the egg and a little of the water and beat to a paste. Gradually whisk in the remaining water.

2 To make the filling, mix together the chicken, soy sauce, shredded cabbage, spring onions, water chestnuts and salt and pepper to taste.

3 Brush a 12 cm (5 inch) omelette or pancake pan with a little oil. Add 1 tablespoon of the batter and tilt the pan to give a thin, even layer. Cook the pancake for about 1 minute then turn it over and cook for 15 seconds. Place on a greased tray. Continue with the remaining batter until you have made 12–14 small pancakes.

4 Lay the pancakes flat and place a spoonful of the filling in the middle of each one. Brush the edge of each pancake with a little egg white. Roll up the pancakes, tucking the ends in firmly and sealing them with a little more egg white if necessary. (The prepared pancakes can be chilled at this stage until needed.)

5 To make the sweet and sour sauce, put all the ingredients except the cornflour and water into a pan and bring to the boil. Mix the cornflour with the cold water and stir into the hot liquid. Return the sauce to the pan and stir over a moderate heat until smooth and thickened.

6 Fill a fondue pot one-third full with oil and heat to 190°C (375°F), or until a cube of bread browns in 30 seconds. Transfer the fondue pot to the table and keep hot over a burner.

7 Carefully lower 2–3 spring rolls at a time into the hot oil and deep-fry for 2–3 minutes until crisp and golden.

8 Provide each person with a plate covered with kitchen paper, and a small bowl of sauce. Garnish with spring onion and red pepper curls, if liked.

Note: To make the spring onion and red pepper curls, cut them into small strips and place in a bowl of iced water for about 1 hour, or until curled.

Serves 4–6
Preparation time: 30 minutes
Cooking time: 40 minutes

MARINATED PORK IN ORANGE FONDUE

750 g (1½ lb) lean pork fillet
1 teaspoon cornflour
1 tablespoon water
vegetable oil, for deep-frying
salt and pepper

Marinade:
grated rind and juice of 1 orange
1 garlic clove, crushed
150 ml (¼ pint) apple juice
2 tablespoons oil
1 teaspoon soft brown sugar

1 Cut the meat into bite-sized pieces. Mix all the marinade ingredients together and marinate the meat for a few hours or preferably overnight. Drain the meat, reserving the marinade, and dry on kitchen paper.

2 Pour the marinade into a saucepan and bring to the boil. Blend the cornflour with the water, stir into the sauce and simmer for 2 minutes. Season with salt and pepper to taste.

3 Fill a fondue pot one-third full with oil and heat on the hob to 190°C (375°F), or until a cube of bread browns in 30 seconds. Transfer the fondue to the table and keep warm over a burner.

4 Spear a piece of meat with a fondue fork and cook it in the hot oil until it is done to your liking. Serve the hot marinade sauce with the meat as a dipping sauce.

Serves 4
Preparation time: 20–30 minutes, plus marinating
Cooking time: 10 minutes

SPICY MEATBALL FONDUE

1 tablespoon sunflower oil
1 onion, finely chopped
500 g (1 lb) very lean minced beef
¼ teaspoon grated nutmeg
¼ teaspoon garlic salt
1 egg, beaten
flour, for shaping
oil, for frying
salt and pepper

To serve:
barbecue sauce
green salad

1 Heat the sunflower oil in a frying pan, add the onion and fry until softened. Leave to cool slightly and then mix with the beef, nutmeg, garlic salt, egg and salt and pepper to taste. With well-floured hands, shape the mixture into small balls.

2 Half-fill a fondue pot with oil and heat on the hob to 190°C (375°F), or until a cube of bread browns in 30 seconds.

3 Carefully transfer the fondue pot to the table and keep warm on a burner. Spear each meatball with a fondue fork and cook in the hot oil for 3–4 minutes or until browned. Serve with barbecue sauce and a green salad.

Serves 4–6
Preparation time: 20 minutes
Cooking time: 20 minutes

ROSEMARY LAMB FONDUE

If you like, the marinade can be heated, thickened with cornflour, and served with the fondue.

750 g (1½ lb) fillet of lamb
vegetable oil, for deep-frying
Cumberland Sauce (see below), to serve

Marinade:
1 garlic clove, crushed
150 ml (¼ pint) red wine
2 tablespoons chopped rosemary
1 tablespoon redcurrant jelly
3 tablespoons oil

1 Cut the lamb into bite-sized pieces. Mix all the marinade ingredients and pour into a large bowl. Add the lamb and mix thoroughly, then cover and leave to marinate overnight in the refrigerator. Drain and dry on kitchen paper; if the meat is wet it will make the oil spit when it is cooking.

2 Half-fill a fondue pot with oil and heat on the hob to 190°C (375°F), or until a cube of bread browns in 30 seconds. Transfer the fondue pot to the table and keep warm over a burner. Divide the lamb between individual plates. Spear the lamb with a fondue fork or skewer and cook it in the hot oil until it is done to your liking. Serve with a bowl of Cumberland Sauce.

Serves 4
Preparation time: 25 minutes, plus marinating
Cooking time: 10 minutes

CUMBERLAND SAUCE

1 orange
1 lemon
250 g (8 oz) redcurrant jelly
75 ml (3 fl oz) red wine
25 g (1 oz) soft brown sugar
1 teaspoon arrowroot or cornflour
salt and pepper

1 Thinly remove the rind, without the pith, from the orange and the lemon. Shred the rind finely into matchstick lengths and place in a saucepan of fast boiling water for 3 minutes. Drain and immerse in cold water for 1 minute. Drain again and set aside.

2 Squeeze the juice from the orange and lemon, strain into a saucepan with the redcurrant jelly and bring to the boil over a low heat. Stir in the wine and sugar and season with salt and pepper to taste. Blend the arrowroot with a little cold water and stir into the sauce. Bring to the boil, stirring all the time until slightly thickened. Finally stir in the blanched citrus rind and serve.

Serves 4
Preparation time: 10–15 minutes
Cooking time: 10–15 minutes

FONDUE BOURGUIGNONNE

750 g (1½ lb) fillet steak
parsley sprigs or lettuce, to garnish
(optional)
groundnut oil, for deep-frying

To serve:
accompanying sauces (see below)
French bread
green salad

1 Cut the fillet steak into 1–2 cm (½–1 inch) cubes. Arrange on 4 individual plates, garnishing the meat with parsley or lettuce, if liked.

2 Half-fill the fondue pot with groundnut oil. Heat the oil on the hob to 190°C (375°F) or until a cube of bread browns in 30 seconds, then transfer the fondue pot to the table and keep warm over a burner.

3 Give each person a plate of cubed steak, a fondue fork for spearing and cooking the steak, and a knife and fork for eating the meat, for those who prefer to be more conventional.

4 Each person can then cook their steak in the hot oil. The length of time depends on how rare or well done they like their meat.

5 Provide a selection of sauces for dipping, a basket of hot French bread and a bowl of green salad.

Sauces
Salsa verde:
Using a food processor or blender, combine 2 tablespoons capers, 4 gherkins, 2 garlic cloves, 4 tablespoons olive oil, 4 tablespoons white wine vinegar, 2 tablespoons roughly chopped parsley, a pinch of caster sugar and salt and pepper to taste.

Horseradish sauce:
Mix together 1 tablespoon grated fresh horseradish, 2 tablespoons lemon juice, a pinch of caster sugar, 150 ml (¼ pint) soured cream and salt and pepper to taste.

Mustard sauce:
Mix together 1 small finely chopped onion, 150 ml (¼ pint) mayonnaise, 1 tablespoon French mustard, ½ teaspoon cayenne pepper and salt to taste.

Serves 4
Preparation time: about 10 minutes, plus making sauces
Cooking time: 10 minutes

BANANA FONDUE

3 bananas
I tablespoon lemon juice
I tablespoon sugar
65 ml (2½ fl oz) single cream
50 g (2 oz) plain chocolate, grated
melon balls or pineapple chunks, to serve

I Purée the bananas in a food processor or blender, or push through a sieve with the back of a metal spoon. Fill a fondue pot one-third full with water. Place the porcelain liner in the pot and heat on the hob. Place the bananas and lemon juice in the pot and heat gently. Add the sugar and cream and, when simmering, gradually add the chocolate.

2 When the chocolate has melted, transfer the fondue pot to the table and keep warm over a burner. Serve with melon balls or pineapple chunks to dip into the fondue.

Serves 2
Preparation time: 10 minutes
Cooking time: 10–15 minutes

APRICOT FONDUE

750 g (1½ lb) dried apricots
200 g (7 oz) sugar
pinch of cinnamon
4 tablespoons apricot brandy
cubes of Pound Cake (see page 57) or
sponge cake, to serve

I Soak the apricots in water until soft, then simmer them in a little water until tender. Purée the apricots in a food processor or blender.

2 Place the apricot purée in a fondue pot. Add the sugar, cinnamon and a little water if the mixture is very thick. Heat gently, then stir in the apricot brandy.

3 Transfer the fondue pot to the table and keep warm over a burner. Serve with cubes of pound cake or sponge cake to dip into the fondue.

Serves 2–4
Preparation time: 10 minutes, plus soaking
Cooking time: 10 minutes

CHOCOLATE ORANGE FONDUE

250 g (8 oz) plain chocolate, broken
into pieces
15 g (½ oz) butter
finely grated rind and juice of 1 orange
1 teaspoon arrowroot or cornflour
2 tablespoons Cointreau or other orange
liqueur

To serve:
ratafia biscuits or macaroons
orange segments

1 Fill a fondue pot one-third full with water. Place the porcelain liner in the pot and heat on the hob. Put the chocolate, butter and orange rind and juice into the pot and heat gently, stirring continuously, until the chocolate has melted.

2 Blend the arrowroot or cornflour with the Cointreau and add to the fondue pot, stirring until thickened.

3 Serve with ratafia biscuits or macaroons and orange segments to dip into the fondue.

Serves 2
Preparation time: 10 minutes
Cooking time: 10 minutes

BLACKCURRANT CREAM FONDUE

250 g (8 oz) blackcurrants, trimmed
125 g (4 oz) sugar
125 g (4 oz) butter
175 ml (6 fl oz) water, plus 1 tablespoon
1 tablespoon cornflour
150 ml (¼ pint) double cream
biscotti or almond cookies, to serve

1 Place the blackcurrants, sugar, butter and the water in a saucepan and let the sugar dissolve over a low heat. Bring to the boil and simmer until the blackcurrants are soft. Allow to cool slightly then sieve the fruit.

2 Blend the cornflour with the 1 tablespoon of water. Pour the fruit purée into a fondue pot and stir in the cornflour mixture. Bring to the boil, stirring, and simmer for 2 minutes. Add the cream. Reheat gently, stirring all the time, but do not allow the mixture to boil.

3 Transfer the fondue pot to the table and keep warm over a burner. Serve with Italian biscotti or almond cookies to dip into the fondue, or spoon the warm fondue over the biscuits on your plate.

Serves 4
Preparation time: 10 minutes
Cooking time: 20 minutes

RASPBERRY MALLOW FONDUE

250 g (8 oz) raspberries, fresh or defrosted if frozen
175 g (6 oz) marshmallows
150 ml (¼ pint) double cream
few drops of lemon juice

To serve:
wafer biscuits
macaroons

1 Put the raspberries in a food processor or blender and liquidize to a purée. Fill a fondue pot one-third full with water. Place the porcelain liner in the pot and heat on the hob. Place the raspberry purée, marshmallows and cream in the pot and heat gently, stirring all the time. Add the lemon juice and reheat, but do not allow to boil.

2 Transfer the fondue pot to the table and keep warm over a burner. Serve with wafer biscuits and macaroons for dipping into the fondue.

Serves 4
Preparation time: 5 minutes
Cooking time: 10 minutes

FRUIT AND CHOCOLATE FONDUE

125 ml (4 fl oz) double cream
250 g (8 oz) plain chocolate, finely chopped
I teaspoon vanilla extract

To serve:
cubes of pound cake (see below)
strawberries
slices of fresh or crystallized apricot

I Fill the fondue pot one-third full with water. Place the porcelain liner in the pot and heat on the hob. (Alternatively, place a heatproof bowl over a saucepan of gently simmering water.) Pour the cream into the bowl and heat gently. As soon as the cream starts to bubble around the edges, turn off the heat and whisk in the chocolate. When the chocolate has melted, add the vanilla and stir well to mix.

2 Transfer the fondue pot to the table and keep warm over a burner. Serve the fondue with cubes of pound cake, strawberries and slices of apricot. Use fondue forks, cocktail sticks or bamboo skewers to dip the cake and fruit into the chocolate fondue.

Serves 6–8
Preparation time: 10–15 minutes
Cooking time: 10 minutes

POUND CAKE

175 g (6 oz) plain flour
½ teaspoon baking powder
250 g (8 oz) butter
250 g (8 oz) sugar
4 eggs

I Lightly grease and flour a 11 x 20 x 7 cm (4½ x 8 x 3 inch) loaf tin. Sift together the flour and baking powder and set aside.

2 Cream the butter and sugar in a bowl until light and fluffy. Add the eggs, one at a time, beating well after each egg. Add a tablespoon of flour if the mixture starts to curdle.

3 Fold in the flour then pour the mixture into the loaf tin. Bake in a preheated oven, 180°C (350°F), Gas Mark 4, for about 45 minutes until golden. To test if the cake is done, insert a skewer into the centre of the cake. The cake is done if the skewer comes out clean.

4 Leave the cake to cool in the tin for 10 minutes, then turn out on to a wire rack to cool completely before serving.

Serves 4–6
Preparation time: 20 minutes
Cooking time: 45 minutes

NUTTY DARK CHOCOLATE FONDUE

100 g (3½ oz) bar Toblerone chocolate
50 g (2 oz) plain chocolate
2 tablespoons double cream
1 tablespoon rum

To serve:
selection of fruit including strawberries, raspberries, cherries and sliced banana, dipped in lemon juice

1 Fill a fondue pot one-third full with water. Place the porcelain liner in the pot and heat on the hob. Break the Toblerone and plain chocolate into the pot and add the cream. Stir until the chocolate has melted. Stir in the rum and continue to heat, stirring, for 1 minute.

2 Transfer the fondue pot to the table and keep warm over a burner. Serve with a selection of fruits and biscuits for dipping, using bamboo skewers to spear the fruit.

Serves 4
Preparation time: 15 minutes
Cooking time: 10 minutes

WHITE CHOCOLATE FONDUE

250 g (8 oz) white chocolate, grated
125 ml (4 fl oz) double cream
1 tablespoon Kirsch

To serve:
strawberries
kiwi fruit

1 Fill a fondue pot one-third full with water. Place the porcelain liner in the pot and add the chocolate and cream. Heat gently, stirring continuously, but do not allow to boil. When melted, stir in the Kirsch.

2 Transfer the fondue pot to the table and keep warm over a burner. Serve with strawberries and chunks of kiwi fruit, using bamboo skewers to spear the fruit.

Serves 2
Preparation time: 5–10 minutes
Cooking time: 10 minutes

CHOCOLATE MINT FONDUE

500 g (1 lb) plain chocolate, grated
2 tablespoons crème de menthe or mint chocolate liqueur
150 ml (¼ pint) double cream

To serve:
raspberries
slices of banana, dipped in lemon juice
chocolate mints

1 Fill a fondue pot one-third full with water. Place the porcelain liner in the pot and heat on the hob. Put the chocolate in the pot and melt over a low heat. Stir in the liqueur and cream and reheat gently, stirring continuously. Do not allow to boil.

2 Transfer the fondue pot to the table and keep warm over a burner. Serve with raspberries, slices of banana and chocolate mints. Use bamboo skewers to spear the fruit.

Serves 6
Preparation time: 10 minutes
Cooking time: 10 minutes

ICE CREAM FONDUE

600 ml (1 pint) coffee ice cream
1 tablespoon brandy
1 tablespoon cornflour

To serve:
chunks of banana, dipped in lemon juice
chocolate sticks

1 Melt the ice cream in the fondue pot. Mix the brandy and cornflour and stir into the pot.

2 Serve the fondue with chunks of banana and chocolate sticks for dipping.

Serves 2
Preparation time: 10 minutes
Cooking time: 10 minutes

DARK FUDGE FONDUE

25 g (1 oz) butter
75 g (3 oz) dark soft brown sugar
175 ml (6 fl oz) milk
1 tablespoon black treacle
1 tablespoon cornflour
2 tablespoons water

To serve:
sponge fingers
chunks of banana, dipped in lemon juice
marshmallows

1 Place the butter and sugar in a saucepan and heat gently until the sugar has dissolved, stirring all the time. Bring to the boil and simmer for 1 minute, still stirring. Stir in the milk and treacle. Blend the cornflour with the water and pour in. Bring to the boil, stirring continuously, and simmer for 2–3 minutes.

2 Pour into a fondue pot, transfer to the table and keep warm over a burner. Serve with sponge fingers, chunks of banana or marshmallows speared on fondue forks or bamboo skewers.

Serves 2
Preparation time: 10 minutes
Cooking time: 10–15 minutes

MOCHA FONDUE

250 g (8 oz) plain chocolate
1 tablespoon instant coffee granules
175 ml (6 fl oz) double cream
1 tablespoon sherry
175 g (6 oz) marshmallows or cubes of
pound cake (see page 57), to serve

1 Grate the chocolate and mix with the coffee granules.
2 Fill a fondue pot one-third full with water. Place the porcelain liner in the pot and heat on the hob. Put the cream into the pot and add the chocolate and coffee mixture. Heat gently, stirring continuously, until the fondue is thoroughly blended and smooth.
3 Stir in the sherry and heat gently. Transfer the fondue pot to the table and keep warm over a burner. Serve with marshmallows or cubes of pound cake to dip into the fondue.

Serves 4
Preparation time: 10 minutes
Cooking time: 10–15 minutes

INDEX